TAKING CHARGE

TAKING CHARGE

*A guide to people management
in today's public sector*

Alan Fowler

INSTITUTE OF PERSONNEL MANAGEMENT

Typesetting by The Comp-Room, Aylesbury
and printed in Great Britain by
Short Run Press, Exeter

INSTITUTE OF PERSONNEL MANAGEMENT
IPM House, Camp Road, Wimbledon, London SW19 4UX
Tel: 081-946-9100   Fax: 081-946-2570
Registered office as above. Registered Charity No. 215797
A company limited by guarantee. Registered in England No. 198002

Contents

This booklet is published by the IPM with the encouragement of the Institute's Public Sector Forum. It aims to fill the need for a framework for managing people in the 'new' public sector. The author is a distinguished practitioner with many years' experience in public service and many IPM and other publications to his credit. The initial planning of the book and the working of some original material was the responsibility of Doug Gummery, IPM's policy adviser, employee relations.

Introduction

The public sector is in the throes of radical change – statutory, economic, and cultural. The effective management of these changes requires the skilful replacement of traditional approaches to the management of people by strategies and practices which contribute to the achievement of the new public sector aims and values. Although new technical and administrative systems are important – for example, in the fields of finance and IT – successful change is ultimately dependent on securing the commitment and competence of the organisation's employees.

In a rapidly changing environment, there is a risk of addressing individual personnel practices without adequate consideration of their interaction, or the effect of each on the overall culture of the organisation. This may be seen, for example, in some organisations' preoccupation with the detailed design of performance-related pay schemes which nevertheless use assessment criteria conflicting with (or failing to reinforce) the organisations' separately determined quality or customer care objectives. The introduction of any new policy or scheme should be based on an assessment of its value to the particular organisation, and not simply copied from another source or adopted as a matter of management fashion ('flavour of the month').

In broad terms, a three-stage approach is needed if the risk of misdirected or uncoordinated action is to be avoided:

- Identify the externally driven changes or influences to which the organisation must repond.
- Determine the implications of these changes for the overall style and objectives of the organisation.
- Decide the personnel strategies and practices needed to achieve the necessary cultural change and meet the objectives.

This book follows that sequence. Section 1 discusses the changes and influences common across the whole public sector:

- local or unit autonomy
- the market: external and internal
- the enabling concept
- resource limitation and value for money
- customer orientation.

Section 2 examines the cultural characteristics of the new public sector organisation. Sections 3–8 look in turn at the following people management functions:

- organisation structures and job design
- resourcing (flexibility in staffing practices)
- performance and quality management
- rewards (pay and benefits)
- training and development
- employee relations.

The relevance of these issues to the problems and opportunities facing organisations in the 'new' public sector will be clear to chief executives, head teachers, trust managers and personnel practitioners alike. Steering the right course in the management of people will be a major ingredient in their success.

This book does not cover a comprehensive list of all personnel functions, since the purpose is to focus on the issues of specific relevance to the public sector in the first half of the 1990s. There are a number of other important topics which the public sector manager or personnel specialist needs to address – such as health and safety, and general employment legislation. But these issues are common to all employers, public and private, and are adequately covered by many other publications.

It also needs to be recognised that the public sector is not a homogeneous institution. Some changes are unique to particular parts of the public sector, such as the split in employer responsibilities in schools between the governors and the local education authority and the relationship between government departments and Next Steps agencies. In other cases, the broad issues are the same, but their detailed regulation differs. For example, market testing in local government is prescribed by statutory regulations for compulsory competitive tendering which differ in detail from those for the NHS or Civil Service. This book does not attempt to deal with detailed variants of this kind. It addresses issues which, in principle or general character, are common across the whole sector.

Section 1
The elements of change

Local or unit autonomy

For many managers, the most direct change is that they now have the authority to make decisions on a range of issues which have previously been determined centrally or nationally. Many welcome this greater freedom of action; some find it daunting; all need to develop new skills.

Widespread devolution, both from the cenfre to individual units and within units themselves, raises important organisational and policy issues. Unplanned devolution can lead to variations in standards which the public may well consider unacceptable and to internal disintegration. Successful devolution requires, as a first step, decisions about the issues for which the organisation as a whole considers it essential to maintain consistency of standards. In the personnel field, this may include such matters as:

- equal opportunities
- trade union recognition
- management development.

Defining the key issues for which devolved units are expected to maintain consistent standards does not imply detailed central control. What is needed is a clear statement of the necessary standards, followed by some form of monitoring. The message to unit managers is: 'You have the freedom to manage your own staff provided you do so well. Managing well means you may adopt whatever personnel practices you consider suit your needs and circumstances, provided they meet the core standards and values.'

Beyond the requirement to meet such standards, unit or section managers may then exercise a wide range of choice in three respects:

- the extent to which they depart from existing standardised practices or procedures
- whether they obtain specialist assistance (e.g. for training) from in-house providers, or buy in these services from external sources, or employ their own specialists
- the extent to which they devolve decision-making authority within their own units.

An essential element in the principle of devolution or local autonomy is the concept of the heads of units as 'managers'. Senior staff who have traditionally seen themselves as professionals have to assume a new role in the management of resources. For many, a necessary precursor to learning new skills is the attitudinal acceptance of being managers – and the cultural stress of this change should not be underestimated.

The market: external and internal

One of the most powerful influences on the structure of

public sector organisations is what can broadly be described as the market principle. This involves a belief that organisational efficiency and effectiveness can best be developed by exposing the delivery of services to the results of competition and consumer choice. It is not the purpose of this book to enter the political debate about this concept. What is important factually is the massive impact market principles are having on managerial roles.

In its most extreme form, market theory results in privatisation – the complete transfer of ownership from the public to the private sector, as has happened in the gas, electricity and water industries. This book does not address this issue, except to note that in organisations designated for privatisation, major personnel implications arise – in particular, the need to keep employees fully informed at every stage of the process and to clarify the extent to which existing staff on their current terms will transfer to the new private sector employer.

The aspect of the market principle examined in this booklet is the market testing and CCT (compulsory competitive tendering) of currently in-house functions. Whether or not the in-house function survives these processes, the specification and ultimate control of the function remains with the public sector client, for instance when hospitals contract out their laundry services.

Market testing has three general implications for the way an organisation is structured and operates:

- In the past, top priority was generally given to the direct management of service delivery, i.e. the contractor or provider role. This priority has now shifted to the client role – specifying service requirements and monitoring the performance of external or internal contractors. Some public sector organisations, trying at almost any cost to preserve in-house contractor units, have failed to provide their client side with adequate managerial resources, or to recognise that management by contract demands new managerial skills.

- Either statutory CCT regulations, or the logic of the principles involved, require the roles of client (purchaser) and in-house contractor (provider) to be clearly separated. This has profound effects on internal managerial relationships, and there is a danger of adversarial attitudes developing between the two sides. The concept to foster is that the most effective client/contractor relationship is a collaborative partnership.
- The commercial approach inherent in the market principle implies a need to adopt many business techniques. The challenge for managers is to apply business acumen without losing the high ethical standards inherent in the concept of public service.

The enabling concept

Linked to the market principle, but with wider implications for bodies such as local authorities, is the concept of the enabling organisation. Looked at narrowly, this involves the cessation of direct service provision and its substitution by contract management. But there is broader interpretation. This sees the public body as a focus for community identity and action, which may include activities going well beyond the letting of contracts:

- joint ventures and partnerships with the private sector to initiate projects which neither sector alone would be able or willing to pursue
- similar arrangements with the voluntary sector, through grant aid, the provision of specialist skills and joint management

- acting as a lobbyist on behalf of the community in dealings with central government, other public bodies, the utility companies and the like.

There are two implications of the enabling concept for the evolution of personnel policies and processes:

- There may be attitudinal barriers to overcome before managers and staff at large become committed to the concept. The traditional public sector ethos is of the self-sufficient organisation with its own powerful set of conventions and characteristics. The enabling concept, on the other hand, requires a willingness to reach outside the organisation to tap ideas and resources from bodies far removed in style and tradition from that of the public sector bureaucracy.
- There is also a need for public sector managers to understand the complex network of systems and structures which influence decisions across UK society – and to develop the skills required in working with other and very varied organisations.

Resource limitations: value for money

There are at least three factors which require all public sector organisations to exercise close control of costs:

- pressure by central government to reduce public expenditure
- the effect of market testing in spotlighting the costs of in-house contractor units and their need to achieve competitive 'prices' if they are to win work against commercial tenderers
- the pressure exerted by the Audit Commission and the

National Audit Office for the public sector to demonstrate efficiency and effectiveness – coupled with the determination of organisations themselves to maximise the value of every pound spent.

Financial constraints place a premium on qualities such as ingenuity and innovation in searching for ever more cost-effective ways of working. Unfortunately, some of the features of traditional public sector bureacracies – such as a rigid adherence to detailed procedures and the importance of precedent – militate against these needs. An audit of blockages to experimentation and innovation may prove a valuable first step towards the creation of an organisation which can produce high-quality outcomes from a very limited resource base.

The need for economy requires a clear distinction between direct costs and overheads – with a strong incentive to reduce the latter in favour of the former. While the reduction of overheads is obviously of great importance, managements need to take a long-term view if certain dangers are to be avoided. Too often, functions such as training fall victim to short-term cost-cutting because inadequate attention is paid to the eventual adverse effect of such savings.

Customer orientation

The discovery of 'the customer' has been one of the most obvious changes in the public sector during the past few years. Institutionalised in the Citizens Charter and encouraged by Chartermark awards, the recognition that the rationale for most public bodies is the provision of services to the public has necessitated a fundamental rethink of many aspects of public sector activity.

Public bodies are consequently introducing structures and systems designed to meet customer needs rather than the convenience of their own administrators. Issues which are being addressed include:

- public accessibility to buildings and services
- plain English documentation
- personal identity (instead of anonymity) of public servants
- all-purpose public enquiry points ('one-stop shops')
- guarantees of service standards
- complaints procedures and compensation.

There are three general issues to consider in the pursuit of customer care:

- Employees become cynical about customer care policies if they see them as little more than window-dressing or sloganising – or if inadequate support is given to the front-line staff on whom much of the public reputation of the organisation depends.
- There are services in which the use of the term 'customer' may be inappropriate. Managers need to be sensitive to public reaction on such matters. Other roles for the public than customer may include citizen, constituent, patient, service user, tax-payer, contributor and partner.
- Staff are unlikely to display genuine care for customers if they do not feel that their employing organisation displays care for its employees. Effective customer care needs to be founded on a base of fair and supportive employment practices.

Section 2
A new culture

In addition to the changes discussed in Section 1, there has been a growing realisation that change itself needs to be accepted as normal. In other words, it is unrealistic to think that once an organisation has adjusted to current pressures, it can look forward to a lengthy period of stability. Change of one kind or another – legislative, economic, political, demographic – must be considered as a permanent feature of organisational life.

This points to the need for the effective organisation to be capable of continual adjustment. Adaptability and flexibility are the necessary characteristics for survival and success. These features contrast starkly with traditional public sector qualities which evolved largely to maintain permanence and consistency of aims and activity.

It is therefore a useful exercise to review the current culture of the organisation against a schedule of the characteristics of static and adaptable organisations:

The static organisation	The adaptable organisation
Unresponsive to external influences	Responsive to external influences
Reaction to external change is usually defensive	Reaction to external change is usually opportunistic
Fails to identify trends in external pressures and takes action only if this becomes inevitable	Spots trends early, and acts before being forced to by circumstances
No regular action to monitor customer needs and views	Constant monitoring of customer needs and views
Reluctance to form joint working relationships with outside bodies	Enthusiasm for collaborative working with outside bodies
Has no clear and articulated vision of its long term goals	Has a clear and articulated vision of its long term goals
Internal focus on adherence to own rules and procedures	External focus and emphasis on action to respond to opportunities and threats
High value placed on precedent: 'How did we do this last time?'	Enthusiasm for fresh thinking: 'What do we want to achieve this time?'
Action driven from the top in a multi-level hierarchy	Clear direction from the top on core and corporate goals; but considerable devolution of decision-making through a flat management structure
Centralised systems of detailed vetting and approval	Central vetting and approval limited to minimum necessary to achieve key corporate goals and values
Structure reflects and reinforces internal professional groups and interests	Structure reflects customer groupings and needs
Organisational emphasis on internal or administrative convenience	Organisational emphasis on customer convenience

Work kept strictly within formal and permanent organisational units	Significant use of interdisciplinary work groups, formed as projects require and disbanded when tasks completed
Lengthy formal process for making even minor changes to structures or staffing	Considerable flexibility to enable structural or staffing changes to be made quickly
Detailed rules and regulations covering every aspect of working life	Rules and regulations limited to those necessary to ensure achievement of key goals and core values
Comprehensive documentation – managers communicate by memo	Documentation kept to necessary minimum – managers communicate face-to-face
Reluctance to depart from formal rules or procedures: compliance is an end in itself	Readiness to alter or depart from rules procedures which inhibit goal achievement
Intolerance of mistakes: when things go wrong 'Who is to blame?'	Tolerance of mistakes which result from well-intentioned initiatives: when things go wrong 'What can we learn?'
Emphasis on 100% accuracy	'Roughly right' often acceptable provided goals are achieved
Reluctance to innovate in case things go wrong	Expectation of innovation, and readiness to change if this proves ineffective
Little attempt to tap ideas and initiative of staff	Active involvement of and consultation with all employees
Training emphasis on professional qualifications	Training emphasis on development of work-oriented competences
Strong sense of status distinctions	Minimisation of status distinctions
Little attention to internal communication. Employees poorly informed of aims and activities	Wide-ranging communication strategy. Employees fully informed of aims, values, achievements

13

Features of the successful management of cultural change are:

- clear articulation of the organisation's mission and core values, with the highly visible commitment of top management
- extensive communication throughout the workforce about the changes which are sought, the reasons for change, and the support which will be provided during the change process
- involvement of all levels of management to cascade information throughout the workforce
- the redesign of systems and structures to ensure compatibility with the targeted change
- the provision of training in new skills
- the use of special events (e.g. launch parties, competitions, awards) to generate interest and enthusiasm, and emphasise key messages
- the use of 'symbols' – new logos, slogans, uniforms – to provide visual evidence of changes in style
- obtaining external recognition (e.g. Charter Mark, Investors In People), partly for external reasons but also because such recognition boosts employee morale and focuses attention on key issues.

The personnel function has a major role to play in the design and implementation of cultural change programmes. Specific activities include:

- the design of employee communication strategies
- identifying training needs and providing, or organising the provision of, the necessary training programmes
- reviewing all personnel policies and procedures to eliminate aspects which might inhibit the targeted changes, and introducing new approaches to reinforce the change objectives.

The personnel function can also monitor the impact of the change programme on employees' attitudes. Senior managers may become enthusiastic about the changes they are implementing, and have an unrealistically optimistic impression of the extent to which these changes are understood by staff at large. A monitoring programme, using periodic employee attitude surveys, can make a major contribution to correcting such misconceptions and indicating the aspects of change which require attention if the change objectives are to be met.

Section 3

Organisation structures and job design

The way work is allocated to individual jobs and sections, and the way the relationships between these jobs and sections are structured, influence how successfully the organisation can adapt to change. Before considering characteristics in the design of jobs and structures in an adaptable organisation, it is helpful to look at the features which have in the past been typical of most public sector bodies.

Organisation structures in the public sector have traditonally been characterised by:

- tall (i.e. multi-level) management hierarchies, with as many as 10 or more levels between the chief executive and staff at the bottom of the hierarchy
- departments or groupings based on professional identity rather than on groups of users or customers
- functions such as finance, legal, and personnel held at the centre of the organisation, often with considerable executive authority. There has been a marked tendency

for such central 'support' departments to develop their own standards and objectives and to see their primary role as ensuring compliance with detailed rules and regulations.

Jobs in traditional structures have been very closely defined, with detailed job descriptions setting out each person's duties, but with little indication of any targeted outcomes or standards. The emphasis has been on detailed procedures, rather than on the primary purpose of the job.

Organisational characteristics of these kinds are very effective in ensuring strong centralised control, preventing variability, and maintaining functions in an unchanging state. The problem is that central direction and stasis are not characteristics which enable an organisation to respond effectively to the rapidly changing environment of the 1990s. So the challenge now is to evolve more flexible structures and jobs, without losing the traditional public sector virtues of probity and service.

There are five principal approaches to the design of adaptable organisations:

- decentralisation
- devolution
- delayering
- teamworking
- output-oriented job descriptions

Decentralisation

Decentralisation needs to be distinguished from devolution. In this book, the following definitions have been adopted:

17

- Decentralisation involves the physical and/or organisational relocation of staff and functions from the centre of the organisation to operational departments or units.
- Devolution is the passing of decision-making authority from higher to lower levels of the hierarchy, or from specialists to line managers.

While these concepts may be pursued simultaneously, there are examples of one existing without the other:

- Some organisations have decentralised most of their finance and personnel specialists to work within service departments. They may not, however, have disbanded a highly prescriptive set of financial and personnel procedures. The specialist staff have been distributed throughout the organisation, but retain their original centralist responsibilities for vetting and approving many even minor management decisions.
- In other cases, the central location of finance and personnel specialists has been retained, but considerable authority has been devolved to line managers to make financial and personnel decisions. The centrally located specialists have changed from being controllers to in-house advisers or consultants, though their physical separation from their internal customers may make this change of role less obvious or effective than is desirable.

In any review of current organisational characteristics, it is therefore worth examining the extent to which measures designed to achieve effective decentralisation may be inhibited by the retention of centralist regulations or, alternatively, whether devolution within a centralised structure would be enhanced by some decentralisation.

A concentration of resources at the centre inhibits any large organisation's ability to get 'close to the customer'. It also starves operational or field units of the immediate support they often need – in terms, say, of financial or personnel inputs – if they are to act quickly to meet some new opportunity or threat.

The decentralisation of previously large central functions is consequently a fairly obvious response, though one which may be resisted initially by the central staff concerned. Two common objections are:

- That the transferred central staff will lose their professional identity. The single personnel officer or accountant in an operational unit, who has previously been surrounded by colleagues from the same profession in a large, central department, can feel occupationally isolated. He or she may also worry about their career opportunities. Who will support their professional development when their immediate manager is no longer a senior personnel or finance manager?
- That the transferred specialist will 'go native', adopting the style and objectives of the service unit regardless of corporate standards or goals and may even collaborate with line management in obstructing the remaining central specialist function.

These dangers need to be addressed. Using the personnel function as a model, the following measures can be suggested:

- A halfway house towards full decentralisation is for the previously centrally located personnel officers to be outposted to work in operational departments, but to remain executively responsible to the central head of personnel. Professional identity and loyalty is thus maintained, but with the advantages of immediate proximity to the personnel function's internal customers.

19

The potential disadvantage is that line managers may see the personnel officer as a 'spy in the camp', and fail to encourage integration within the service management team. Some organisations, however, have succeeded with this approach, or have used it for a period while easing into full decentralisation on a phased basis.

- The central head of personnel, while having no executive control over the decentralised personnel officers, retains a 'head of profession' role. Departments' personnel officers are members of their operational department's management teams and report directly to the relevant line managers. The central head of personnel, however, has a continuing functional responsibility to ensure the professional competence and development of all personnel staff. To do so, he or she has career development discussions with each departmental personnel specialist, discusses their performance with their line managers, and arranges specialist training for them. Regular meetings are also held under the head of personnel's chairmanship which bring all the decentralised personnel staff together to consider current personnel issues. In these ways, the constructive aspects of professionalism are maintained, and the isolation of the single decentralised personnel officer reduced.
- The job descriptions of decentralised personnel officers can include a requirement to advise their line managers on the implementation of corporate personnel policies or standards. Line managers then need to be helped to recognise that the service provided by their personnel specialists is not solely to support departmental activities, but also to ensure that all parts of the organisation are successful in meeting relevant corporate objectives.

Organisations embarking on decentralisation may

experience contractual difficulties if their employees' contracts of employment are too narrowly drawn. An appointment letter which states: 'You will be employed as a . . . *job title* . . . in the . . . *xyz* . . . department in the office at . . . *location* . . .', prevents a transfer in the same job but to another department in a different location unless the employee agrees. Ideally, any transfer would have the support of the employee concerned, but when it is decided to decentralise on any scale, the agreement of every single employee cannot be taken for granted. Organisations wishing to secure flexibility are well advised to include a mobility clause in their contract documentation, such as:

> You will initially be employed as a . . . *job title* . . . in the . . . *xyz* . . . department in the office at . . . *location* . . . but you may be required at any time to transfer to another suitable post in any other of the organisation's departments or locations.

The practicability of decentralisation is directly influenced by size. A small central personnel unit with, say, only three professional staff cannot easily be dispersed into the organisation's various operational departments. The test is: can the central function be split into sufficient workable units to be transferred to operational departments, while still leaving at the centre whatever core of expertise the organisation needs to meet its corporate objectives?

Devolution

Devolution is not affected by size. It is as feasible to devolve decision-making authority within the management structure of an organisation with less than 100 employees, as it is within an organisation with a workforce of thousands. It is also a concept which can be applied below the management structure, with wider authority delegated to even basic grade staff. Many public sector organisations have restructured systems and jobs to enable staff in direct contact with the public to give a more comprehensive service.

The principal aims of devolution are therefore:

- to enable decisions to be made as close as possible to the point at which the need for the decision occurs
- to improve the speed and sensitivity of the organisation's response to its customers' needs
- to make maximum use of the detailed knowledge and expertise which exists within each level or section of the workforce
- to develop a greater sense of interest and commitment within the workforce, particularly below the senior management level
- to facilitate the simplification of management structures.

Devolution in a personnel context has two components:

- The authority to make decisions on many employment issues is devolved from senior to less senior levels in the management hierarchy. For example, unit or section managers, who previously had to seek top management approval for any recruitment, may now be free to decide their unit's staffing, limited only by an overall budget within which there is freedom to trade off staff costs against non-personnel costs.
- Decision-making authority is also transferred from the personnel function to line management. This involves changes to personnel procedures. For example, there may have been a system which required all proposals to

allocate leased cars to be vetted and approved by the personnel department. In a devolved system, these decisions may be made by line managers (albeit within guidelines).

Devolution from personnel specialists to line managers has a very specific purpose – to focus attention on the concept that the most important part of every manager's job is the management of people. In the traditional public sector system, when difficult personnel situations arose – concerning discipline or industrial relations, for example – managers could refer the problem to the personnel department and act as though such matters were extraneous to their principle tasks. In a devolved system, managers quickly realise that skilful staff management is the key to all-round managerial effectiveness, and that to be seen by their staff as the person making most employment decisions strengthens their leadership role.

There are, however, two major concerns about the extensive devolution of personnel decisions:

- Have line managers the knowledge and skills necessary to handle this important aspect of their jobs effectively? Managers who have been promoted primarily on the basis of their expertise in very different professional contexts may be seriously lacking in the competencies needed to handle activities such as selection interviewing, conducting discipline enquiries and negotiating with trade unions.
- In an organisation of any size, how can an acceptable level of consistency be maintained in the standards of employment practice, when numerous line managers each have a large degree of decision-making autonomy?

The first problem can be addressed by training (see

23

Section 7), and it needs to be recognised that successful devolution requires a significant training investment. The second problem does not have so obvious a solution, though recentralisation (the response of some organisations) is an admission of defeat. A four element approach is indicated:

- The organisation as a whole must decide the features of its employment activities for which it is considered essential to maintain consistency of standards or principles. Successful devolution has been described as 'freedom within boundaries' – and it is for the organisation itself, not its separate units or devolved managements, to determine what these boundaries are.
- Meeting corporately determined employment standards must then be incorporated into every manager's set of objectives, and performance against these standards should be part of a regular appraisal or monitoring process.
- The personnel function at the core of the organisation contributes to this approach in two ways:
  - by advising top management on the personnel issues which require corporate standards
  - by monitoring the extent to which the targeted standards are being met and are effective.
- Decentralised personnel staff, working to their various line managers, also have two functions:
  - helping their managers apply the corporate standards to the specific employment situations within their units
  - evolving and helping to operate the personnel processes for which there is full devolved freedom.

This approach does not imply the continuation of conventional central prescription of detailed personnel procedures. What the core of the organisation defines are principles and standards – not the detailed mechanisms by which these requirements can be met. Two examples illustrate the approach:

- The organisation may state a simple requirement that all employees must be within a performance appraisal process. In addition, it may be specified that this process must comply with the following principles:
  - appraisal discussions between every manager and his or her staff must be held at least annually
  - the appraisal must consider both job performance and each employee's training and development needs
  - each appraisal must review past performance and future objectives
  - all appraisal records must be open to the employees concerned.

  It will then be left to each departmental or unit manager, advised by the decentralised personnel staff, to operate whatever detailed appraisal system best suits that unit's circumstances – provided all such systems across the organisation meet this simple set of basic principles.
- Managers of departments or units may be given the devolved authority to recruit and select their own staff, but the organisation states that, in the interests of effective recruitment, the selection process in all units must include at least two techniques in addition to normal interviews. It is then for each unit, with professional personnel advice, to decide which particular selection techniques are best for its types of jobs.

Delayering

Delayering – the stripping out of whole levels of management – often goes with devolution. Once section managers have been given greater decision-making authority, the need for intermediate levels of management between them and top management needs to be questioned. The other objective is financial – the reduction of managerial overheads.

Analysis of the role of each management level may well reveal scope for simplifying the organisation structure. Three features are worth close scrutiny:

- Deputy appointments which have no specific function other than to act as a managerial filter between their senior managers and other staff – i.e. a one-to-one, chief-to-deputy relationship. This type of structure is often a symptom either of the job being too large (in which case a better solution is to split it, not to interpose the additional level of a deputy), or of a traditional style of management in which the top manager remained relatively remote from day-to-day management and left 'running the shop' to the deputy.
- Any part of the structure in which a manager has only a very few subordinates. Very narrow spans of management inevitably lead to tall (multi-level) hierarchies.
- A study of what each management tier contributes to the output of the organisation in addition to allocating work to the next lower level and monitoring that level's performance. The justification for the existence of a management tier should be that it adds value – not just that it supervises the work of others.

Implementing a delayering programme can be a painful process as it generally involves job losses, particularly among middle managers. The full range of measures to avoid compulsory redundancies can be applied – redeployment, retraining, seeking volunteers for redundancy, and early retirement. Should enforced redundancies prove inevitable, outplacement counselling and any action which assists displaced managers in finding other work should be given as high a priority as financial compensation.

Teamworking

A common characteristic of the adaptable organisation is the use of multi-skilled teams, drawn from across departmental boundaries, to address specific issues and be disbanded when each project is complete. Effective project teams are concerned only with the contribution each member can make to the task in hand – not to grade or status distinctions. Every member of a project team should be treated equally, regardless of the probable differences in the salary or status which derive from their basic jobs.

Teamworking should be seen not just as an effective way of addressing specific tasks, but also as excellent developmental experience for the team members. Leading a project team may provide an able young professional with invaluable experience of work planning and leadership to aid the difficult transition from the role of specialist to that of manager. For all team members, working across departmental boundaries develops a broader understanding of the interrelationships between various functions, and enhances corporate identity.

On a more permanent basis, the restructuring of an organisation may usefully involve the grouping together of previously separate functions if analyses show that cross-functional working has become frequent, or would improve the quality of customer service. This approach may be adopted for the personnel function. In organisations which have introduced the concept of internal consultancy services, it may prove beneficial to the users of these services to establish multi-professional consultancy teams, instead of each function (including personnel) operating separately. A team or consultancy unit might then be staffed by personnel, IT, finance and management services specialists to provide the same breadth of expertise as is offered by many commercial consultancies.

Output-oriented job descriptions

Public sector job descriptions have had two characteristics which operate against the development of an adaptable organisation:

- They have normally listed the duties or activities in the work in considerable detail, without stating the overall purpose (or output) of the job.
- By including job descriptions in the documentation issued on the appointment of new employees, they have often been incorporated into contracts of employment – wittingly or otherwise.

The effect has been to encourage rigid adherence to detailed procedures, and so discourage employees from taking intiatives to improve working methods or outcomes. Treating job descriptions as part of the employment contract may also make changes to working methods difficult to introduce, or place the price tag of a pay rise on even quite minor job changes.

In the adaptable organisation, job descriptions emphasise what the job is there to do. How this objective or job purpose is met (i.e. in terms of procedures) is of less importance, and it is recognised that the detailed content of the job may well need to change from time to time. To illustrate this, the following examples show part of an accountant's job description before and after the principles of flexibility and job purpose were applied:

- Before: 'Responsible for producing monthly budget variation statements in accordance with the procedure set out in Financial Regulations'.
- After: 'To assist budget-holders to operate within budget by informing them of budget variations and advising them on means of adjusting expenditure'.

Some organisations refer to descriptions of job purpose as 'accountability statements', and use a standard format in these definitions. This has three components:

- An action verb
- The object of the action
- The desired result (outcome)

For example, the accountability statement for a safety officer might be:

> To monitor (*action verb*) hazards and safety measures (*objects of action*) and evolve and implement (*action verbs*) new measures (*object of action*) in order to reduce the accident rate to below the sector average (*result or outcome*).

The details of how the job is done is either omitted, or listed separately as a guide to any newly appointed employee.

If a detailed schedule of work procedures is issued, it should be made clear that this is done to assist the employee to understand the job as it is currently done, but that methods may change and such changes will not constitute alterations to the contract of employment. A

29

statement along the following lines may be included in the appointment documentation:

> The enclosed list of current duties is issued as a guide to help you understand the work you will initially be required to undertake. It may be changed from time to time to meet changing circumstances. It does not form part of your contract of employment.

The impact of market testing and the internal market

At the heart of the market concept is the distinction between two roles – the purchaser (or client) and the provider (or contractor). This division may apply to whole organisations or establishments – e.g. GP fund-holder (purchaser) and hospital (provider) – or to units within a single organisation – e.g. a local authority housing department (client) purchasing maintenance work from the same authority's in-house contractor or Direct Service Organisation (DSO).

In practice, roles and relationships are often much more complex than this simple two function model. Thus:

- A distinction can be drawn between the legally binding contractual relationships between an organisation as client and a private sector contractor and the non-binding quasi-contractual relationships between a client department and an in-house provider (e.g. an operational department 'buying' specialist services from the in-house personnel unit).
- For some functions, it may be a statutory requirement to apply market testing; for others, this is no more than a managerial option. Another possibility is to abandon any attempt to win contracts for the in-house function and, instead, to concentrate entirely on the client role.

- An organisation whose overall role is as a provider (e.g. a hospital or Civil Service agency) may itself be a purchaser of sub-contracted services; and may also apply the internal market principle to the organisation of its support functions such as personnel, finance or IT.

The principal organisational implications of the market concept apply most powerfully to organisations whose in-house functions include both the purchaser and provider roles. This requires a clear division between the roles to be made at some point in the hierarchy. Managerial logic (and in some cases, statutory regulations) make it impracticable to operate twin-role units under 'twin-hatted' managers. This leads to units or functions which conventionally have not distinguished between the two roles being split into separate units.

This does not pose major problems when the two functions are as occupationally or professionally distinct as housing management (purchaser) and housing maintenance (provider), or when the purchaser/client is the organisation corporately and the provider/contractor is as distinct and limited a function as staff catering or office cleaning.

The separation of purchaser and provider within the same function is more difficult – and this is an issue of increasing importance to the personnel function itself. In local government, statutory regulations are being prepared which will require a set percentage of the total personnel activity (and of most other white collar functions) to be put to competitive tender. Other public sector bodies, such as Post Office Counters, are taking similar action voluntarily. Additionally, many organisations have decided to introduce internal trading, and now see their personnel units (together with other central support functions) as business units, 'selling' their services as providers to service management purchasers. This raises an important question: is the personnel function in such an organisation solely a provider, or is there a personnel purchaser or client role?

What some organisations have decided is that the purchaser/provider model is too simple a concept for functions such as personnel and finance if it is interpreted as implying that the whole function has to be either one or other of these two roles. There is also a recognition that the corporate management of the organisation fits uneasily into the quasi-commercial characteristics of the purchaser role.

Four different roles are emerging from such considerations, plus a sub-function within the client role (described on the next page):

- a *core role*: the determination of corporate values, standards , strategies and goals
- a *programme development role*: taking the core objectives and applying these to the organisation's various activities in order to produce specific plans and programmes
- a *client role*: converting the programmes into detailed specifications for the letting of contracts to external or internal providers
- a *provider or contractor role*: the in-house delivery of the services set out in the specifications.

This does not mean that in every case each role is undertaken by different people. The core and programme roles, or the programme and client roles, may well be combined – depending on the size of the function and the volumes of work involved within each role. It is proving helpful, however, to distinguish these various roles, even if in some cases one person may be undertaking more than one.

The provider/contractor role does not lend itself to any combination with other roles. If a unit is to operate as an actual or quasi contractor, it needs to concentrate wholly on marketing the services it can offer, developing its trading relationships with its clients, and producing the fee income it needs to cover its costs.

Applied to the personnel function, this role analysis is helpful due to its recognition of the core and programme roles. If the organisation follows the devolution principle of freedom within boundaries, it needs a top level personnel input within the core to help identify the personnel standards and strategies required to meet its overall human resource objectives and to convert these into specific principles and programmes.

Some organisations see this type of personnel activity as a provider function, with the corporate core of the organisation as the client. The emerging view, however, (and one more in accord with proven private sector practice) is that this activity is better seen as an integral element of the core itself. It can then be combined with the client role – acting for the core in the specification and purchasing of specific personnel services either from an in-house business unit, or from external sources. The importance and influence of the core personnel role is wholly unrelated to its size. It is not a role requiring a large staff – in some organisations it is being undertaken by a single person, with a separate in-house personnel provider unit under its own business unit manager. On an organisation chart, these roles may appear as in the diagram overleaf.

A sub-function of the client role was referred to above. This is being termed 'client agent' by the organisations which have developed the concept. Managers heading the various operational departments have to 'buy' personnel and financial services from the in-house providers or business units, often through service level agreements.

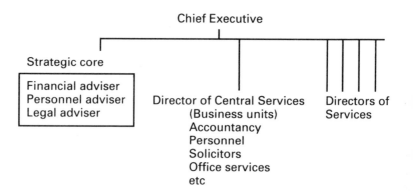

Chief Executive

Strategic core

Financial adviser
Personnel adviser
Legal adviser

Director of Central Services
(Business units)
Accountancy
Personnel
Solicitors
Office services
etc

Directors of
Services

So the operational department is the client. The question arises, how can managers without their own personnel or financial expertise specify the best solutions to meet their human resource or financial needs? It is a confusion of roles if they have to rely on the expertise and advice of the provider. The emerging concept is that this can be corrected by the core specialist acting as the client on behalf of the non-specialist purchaser. To take an example:

- A housing department without its own personnel officer needs to specify and pay for the personnel services it requires from an in-house personnel business unit. There may also be devolved authority to purchase some of these services externally. The organisation has a small personnel unit within the core which has a core/programme role for the organisation as a whole (as in the organisation chart, above). So the housing department seeks the assistance of this unit in determining and specifying its personnel service requirements. In undertaking this activity, the core personnel unit is acting as an agent of the housing client – hence 'client agent'.

Some organisations may consider this role analysis to

be too complex. Deciding the right organisational structure depends on a variety of factors, of which style, size, the range of activities involved, and the level of managerial competence are only some. There is no standard, correct or best model. One of the most important and strategic personnel functions is contributing to organisational analysis and development – which is why this section has devoted so much space to a discussion of organisational principles.

Section 4
Resourcing

Employment practices in the public sector have been characterised by their lack of flexibility. Most employees are full-time staff on open-ended contracts, while overtime, shift work, standby and call-out arrangements are governed by often complex rules and arrangements for extra payments. Staffing levels and structures have also been subject to detailed and centralised control, sometimes with arbitrary limits set on head counts.

This type of resourcing creates considerable rigidity, with costs and delays in adjusting staffing levels to meet changes in the nature or volume of work. There is consequently a need to identify measures which will inject more flexibility into the employment system. In this search for flexibility, the devolution of personnel decisions to line managers is of assistance. Managers should, for example, be able to form and reform teams quickly and to make reasonable changes to job content without having to seek approval 'up the line' or from a central personnel department. But this alone will not fully address the issue. Five additional points are examined in this section:

- the core and periphery concept
- variety in types of employment
- non-employed resources
- flexibility in working times
- equal opportunity and legislative implications.

Core and periphery

One possible approach to meeting the needs of the adaptable organisation is that of a small, stable core of skilled managers and professionals, surrounded by an outer ring made up of a wide variety of work providers (internal and external) whose services can readily be increased or reduced. Although this core and periphery model was originally developed in a private sector context (particularly by Professor Charles Handy of the London Business School), market testing and CCT has made it increasingly relevant to the public sector. In relation to the roles set out in Section 3, the core would consist of the core/programming/client roles, while the periphery would consist of the providers.

The match of the theoretical model with reality is not perfect. For example, most provider organisations of any significant size may have their own cores and outer rings of sub-contractors. Some elements of staffing flexibility are also applicable to core employees. But the general concept can be useful in deciding whether, where, and how best to introduce a variety of types of resourcing.

Variety in types of employment

Three questions should be asked before any vacant post is filled or new post created:

- Is the work involved essential? (What would be the consequences of leaving the post unfilled?)
- If the work is essential, are there less costly or more flexible employment options other than the appointment of a full-time employee on a permanent contract?
- Alternatively, might it be better for the work to be done by an external provider?

Various options are outlined below.

Part-time employment for a fixed five-day schedule
Close study of many jobs may well reveal that the work involved does not require a precise 35 or 37 hours' work each week. There are savings to be made even by 'long' part-time hours, say, 25 to 30 per week.

Part-time employment of full daily hours for only some days each week
There are some work routines which peak on certain days or in which one day a week is extremely slack. Part-time employment for between one and four full days each week is then worth consideration.

Part-time employment with variable weekly hours
This may include a requirement to work an average of, say, 15 hours per week over each month, but the hours worked each day or week may fluctuate to meet changing work requirements.

Employment with no hours specified
The contractual obligation is to complete a specified task or volume of work each week or other set period, not to work for any set time. For example, a finance unit may contract with a person to produce a monthly cost analysis. It is estimated that this involves approximately 40 hours'

work per month, and a monthly salary is set pro rata to this amount. However, the contract of employment states that this monthly sum will be paid 'for the satisfactory production of the cost analysis by the last Friday of each month' and the employee concerned is free to decide when and for how long to work – provided the analysis is produced on time.

Employment during school term times

Contracts with only term-time duration have commonly been used for some support staff in schools, colleges and education authority offices. They suit the domestic needs of working parents who need to be at home with their children during school holidays. There may be jobs unconnected with education where such arrangements would also be practicable.

Contracts for performance

This is the legal term for contracts which state that employment will cease on completion of a specified task or when certain circumstances arise, without this final date being known. This type of employment arrangement suits project work and other circumstances in which it seems probable that the need for a job will disappear when a particular situation arises. An example might be:

> This employment will cease on the date at which the new computer facility is formally transferred from the development team to the Computer Operations Unit.

Fixed term contracts

This type of contract, which unlike contracts for performance has a predetermined duration, has become increasingly used for senior managerial jobs. The reason for this is not always obvious, except for a general view that it provides a periodic opportunity to review the suitability of the job-holder for continued employment. These contracts have a more obvious use when the date of completion of a project (or some other reason for the end of employment) is known in advance.

Temporary employment
Legally, temporary employment falls into one or other of the previous two categories (or, if lasting too long, gives the employees concerned the same legal rights as 'normal' employment). In practice, however, the term is generally used for employees taken on for relatively short periods to cover seasonal work peaks or one-off tasks of fairly short duration.

Standby or supply employment
The education service has long used a system of 'supply teachers' – a register of teachers who can be called in at short notice to provide cover for absent full-time teaching staff. There may be opportunities to develop a similar system for some other types of work to avoid the overtime costs of meeting temporary work peaks. It may prove necessary, however, to pay standby workers a small retainer while they are not working in order to ensure their availability on the supply register.

Weekend or evening shifts
For work requiring attendance beyond the normal five-day, 9-to-5 pattern, it may prove less costly than conventional rotating shift working to cover the additional hours by a separate workforce recruited to work only at weekends or evenings on plain-time rates.

Job sharing
The arrangement for two (or even more) people to take

responsibility for one job can provide considerable flexibility in coping with work fluctuations and short absences – provided the two persons concerned establish a collaborative working relationship.

Non-employed resources

Direct employment always has an element of rigidity, in that employees cannot and should not be hired or fired at will. More flexibility may be obtained by certain tasks being done other than by employment. The main options are described below.

Self-employed persons
In Inland Revenue jargon, these are sole traders. For legal and tax reasons, it is not possible simply to persuade the generality of existing employees to give up their employed status and become self-employed. However, there are often specific tasks or services for which it would be legitimate to use self-employed persons. These are activities for which, once a specification has been produced, the organisation need not exercise control over the methods used by the provider or his or her working time – though providers must satisfy the Inland Revenue that they are operating as genuine businesses. This involves being free to accept or reject the work which is offered, providing their own facilities, having more than one customer, and taking all the normal financial business risks. They must not, of course, be paid holiday or sick pay by the client organisation or be subject to normal employee direction and discipline.

Contractors and consultants
The use of contractors and consultants has grown significantly in recent years. This has been due partly to

market-testing, partly to organisations reducing direct employment to a basic minimum to cut costs. In the personnel and training field, there are now some 5000 consultancies listed in the relevant directories, and specialist services can be obtained from these sources for:

- recruitment and selection
- executive search
- recruitment advertising
- psychometric testing
- distance learning
- all forms of training and development
- health and safety
- equal opportunities
- employee counselling
- relocation
- reward systems and job evaluation
- attitude surveys
- cultural analysis
- pensions
- personnel computer systems
- employee catering
- employee communications
- legal services
- childcare.

There are also the advisory and consultative services of ACAS, and sources of information and advice such as those provided by the IPM. Some managers feel it is an admission of weakness to use consultants. A more positive view is to see consultants as providing a wider range of potential resources than any single organisation could ever sustain internally, if it is clear what the organisation requires and the quality to be specified.

Joint ventures and partnership working
The concept of the totally self-contained organisation needs to be challenged. It may result in a duplication of effort with a similar or related organisation, and it also fails to exploit the advantages which may accrue from two or more organisations pooling their expertise and resources. Joint or partnership working with other organisations can increase flexibility both by avoiding the need to recruit new staff and by enlarging the resource base. But partnership may also require compromises if the objectives of both organisations are to be encompassed.

Examples of joint working by personnel units include:

- management development programmes run jointly by the organisation and a local college or university
- psychometric testing services being provided by one organisation (say, a local authority) for a group of others
- a consortium of organisations operating a recruitment advertising agency and so obtaining commissions and discounts which none could have obtained on their own
- a group of organisations pooling their training facilities to run a single training centre.

Flexibility in working times

In addition to using different types of employment, flexibility can be enhanced by reducing the reliance on fixed daily and weekly working times. The main variants are described below.

Flexible working hours
Flexible hours systems have been in use for many years, mainly in an office context. While the detail may vary,

43

they are all based on the principle of requiring daily attendance during a period of 'core time' (say, between 10 am and 4 pm) and permitting employees to start and finish work within a much wider range of hours (say, 8 am to 10 am start and 4 pm to 7 pm finish). Actual attendance over an accounting period (usually one month) is also required to total at least the equivalent of a standard schedule of weekly hours. Hours in excess of this total may usually be taken as a whole or part days off – 'flexi-leave'.

There has been some disillusionment about flexible hours in recent years, mainly because of the following flaws:

- staff failing to clock off during the lunch break, in schemes which use mechanical time recording systems
- staff who ensure they always work sufficient extra hours to be able to take a day's leave every month, perhaps by coming in to work early before a supervisor is present. The resultant loss of 12 full days attendance is not fully offset by what may be the relatively unproductive extra hours worked
- the administrative work involved in maintaining detailed time and attendance records.

Rather than abandon the use of flexible hours because of these shortcomings, the use of the simplest possible system, backed by effective attendance management by supervisors, and with only a very limited facility to take flexi-leave, may well enable the organisation to obtain the benefits without experiencing significant difficulties.

Variable hours on a seasonal basis
Some functions (e.g. grounds maintenance, outdoor leisure facilities) have a distinct seasonal pattern. Rather than working to the same weekly schedule throughout the year,

it is preferable to use two schedules: e.g. November to March, 32 hours; April to October, 39 hours; giving an annual average of 36. This prevents under-utilisation in the winter and overtime payments in the summer.

Annual hours contracts
These contracts specify the total number of hours to be worked annually, and can provide far more flexibility – though they are complex to plan and manage. The annual total of, say, 1800 hours is made up of variable work schedules to meet operational requirements (including evening or weekend work at non-premium rates) plus, in many cases, some additional hours reserved for unforeseen requirements. Most schemes place limits on the maximum number of hours which can be worked in any week (say, 55), and provide for guaranteed time off. It is advisable to obtain specialist assistance if introducing an annual hours scheme, as there are many possible variants. Some organisations, too, have experienced considerable industrial relations difficulties in the introduction and operation of these schemes.

Home-based working
Employees working at or from their homes are contracted simply to undertake certain tasks and meet prescribed output targets. No control is exercised over the time they choose to spend on their work, though for pay purposes, a view has to be taken as to whether they are, in effect, full or part time employees. The range of functions for which home-based working may be practicable has widened considerably with the development of office technology. Equipped with a PC, modem, electronic mail, telephone and fax, an outworker is now able to keep in close contact with the office – though technology is no substitute for informal face-to-face communication. One way of combatting the

sense of isolation which some home-based employees experience is to provide an office base, shared by several outworkers, and to ensure that regular office visits are paid to meet colleagues and management, and to discuss work issues.

Although not yet widely used, homeworking does offer considerable flexibility, provided the possible problems of loss of contact and supervision are addressed. Fluctuations in workload are much more readily addressed by staff who are not tied to office-based attendance times, and cost savings include some office overheads as well as overtime.

Equal opportunity and other legal implications

From an equal opportunities viewpoint, the adoption of flexibility measures needs very careful consideration. Aspects which can contribute to meeting equal opportunities objectives are those which provide employment opportunities for persons (mainly women) who because of domestic responsibilities cannot take up full-time or office-based jobs.

Care needs to be taken, however, to guard against the following potentially adverse features:

- Part-time staff being treated less favourably in terms of pay, conditions and access to training than full-timers. If, as is probable, the proportion of women among part-timers is significantly higher than among full-timers, any less favourable treatment could well constitute unlawful indirect discrimination.
- Current UK law provides less protection for 'short' part-time employees than for those working 16 hours or more per week.

- Problems under annual hours contracts relating to frequently changing attendance requirements, which disadvantage more women than men. It may not be possible for employees to change their childcare arrangements sufficiently quickly (or variably) to match the employer's requirements for variations in attendance times.

There are also some legal pitfalls to be aware of:

- So-called temporary employees acquire full statutory employment rights once they have two years' continuous service. Designating an employee as a temporary has no legal effect in this respect.
- A temporary or casual worker may acquire continuity of employment despite some breaks in paid employment (e.g. during school holidays) if the breaks are caused by 'a temporary cessation of work' – a phrase not defined in the statute – or if the person is 'regarded by the employer as continuing in employment for any or all purposes' – another undefined phrase. There have been numerous legal cases about this issue, and specialist advice is desirable before introducing any temporary employment scheme in which breaks are planned or probable.
- The expiry and non-renewal of a fixed term contract constitutes dismissal. Normal unfair dismissal and redundancy rights then accrue unless the contract is for two years or more and includes a clause by which the employee agrees to waive these rights.

Section 5

Performance and quality management

Restrictions on public expenditure, the Citizens' Charter movement, and rising public expectations, have resulted in attention being focused on two key issues:

- cost-effectiveness of services – or value for money
- the quality of services, including the need to define the quality standards the public should expect.

While all managers would agree that achieving value for money and consistency of quality have always been managerial objectives, these general aims have not always been supported by a systematic or procedural framework. It has also been evident that in some organisations, a failure to define corporate aims and standards has left individual managers to decide for themselves which aspects of performance and quality to pursue. The result has sometimes been conflict or inconsistency between different parts of the same organisation.

While decisions about performance objectives and

quality standards are clearly a matter for managements as a whole (and may in some institutions such as local government be a matter for political direction), the personnel function has a major role to play in helping to evolve and implement new systems to support these aims. The reason for an emphasis on the human dimension is that the achievement of high levels of performance and quality depends crucially on the competence and motivation, not just of senior managers, but of the whole workforce.

Performance management

The basic principles of a comprehensive performance management system are:

- The organisation defines its corporate mission (its fundamental purpose), core values (the qualities it wishes to see upheld throughout all its activities), and long- and short-term priorities.
- Each department of the organisation then applies these corporate aims and standards to its own activities, adds items which are specific to its own function, and so produces a set of departmental objectives.
- The same process is cascaded down to sub-units and teams.
- Objectives (variously termed goals or targets) are then evolved for each employee. These are specific to the purpose and tasks within each job, but support sectional, departmental and corporate aims and values.
- At each level, action plans are produced to ensure the objectives are met.
- There are periodic reviews of achievement against objectives, and new or revised objectives and action plans are then produced for the next review period.

Despite the logic of these principles, research into performance management systems has often failed to find hard evidence of their effectiveness. Four reasons for failure are:

- systems which are seen by line managers as impositions, originating from central specialists in finance, personnel or management services units. Managers rarely operate a performance management system well unless they feel a sense of ownership, and see the system as an integral and helpful part of their own management processes
- a failure to develop an integrated approach – i.e. systems with only a patchy coverage of the organisation or which fail to link all objectives to unifying corporate aims and values
- an over-emphasis when setting objectives on just one aspect – particularly cost-cutting – sometimes because it is thought too difficult to define broader, qualitative goals
- systems requiring a large volume of additional paperwork and administration in their operation.

The aspects of performance management which many managers find most difficult are objective setting and performance measurement, and appraisal interviewing. These are examined below.

Setting and measuring objectives

Objectives for individual employees should be:

- reasonable aspirations for competent and well-motivated staff to achieve
- not so easily achieved that they become discredited

- clearly dependent on the performance of the employee concerned, provided any necessary support or resources have been provided
- related to the core values, priorities and objectives of the organisation as a whole and of the section in which the employee works
- capable of measurement or assessment in achievement
- revised quickly, if unexpected circumstances require changes, or make the original objectives impracticable.

There is little point in setting objectives for which no form of measurement or assessment can be applied. For many managers this poses perceived problems. They hold that while the private sector can readily set measurable commercial objectives (i.e. profitability), many public service functions cannot be assessed so precisely because of their inherently qualitative features. This view is based on a misunderstanding of private sector practice, and does not address the necessity of assessing standards of performance in every job – whether or not that performance is susceptible to statistical measurement.

Although the overall performance of a company can be measured by statistical indices such as market share and profit, generally only top managers have such measures built into their personal performance objectives. The generality of employees have other types of objectives specific to their jobs, and these frequently include qualitative as well as quantitative factors. For example, training officers in companies are not set profit targets or appraised solely on training costs: they are judged on the quality and relevance of the training they provide – the same criteria as apply to their public sector counterparts.

The following schedule suggests a categorisation of five broad types of performance indicators, ranging from the largely subjective to the clearly objective:

- *Descriptive opinion:* the informed views of the employee's senior managers, and/or of customers or colleagues, about qualitative aspects of performance – e.g. views of the attitude the employee displays in contacts with the public.
- *Judgemental scales:* a more systematic way of handling largely subjective opinion, as in public opinion surveys in which respondents are asked to indicate their views on specific topics on a rating scale. Public sector organisations are making increasing use of this type of survey to obtain customer satisfaction ratings, and the same approach can be adopted internally. For example, some personnel departments periodically ask line managers to rate the quality or relevance to them of each personnel function (recruitment, training etc.).
- *Ratios:* a wide variety of statistical indicators can be used; e.g. complaints per 1000 transactions, ratio of clerical to operational staff, number of transactions completed per employee per week etc.
- *Time factors:* such as completion of tasks against deadlines, and durations of standard transactions.
- *Financial indicators:* such as unit or transaction costs, income generation, expenditure against budgets.

Appraisal

All systematic performance management includes periodic appraisal discussions between each employee and his or her manager. Appraisal interviewing, done well, contributes to employee motivation and leads to improved performance. Handled badly, it can generate resentment, fear or cynicism. The following schedule shows the characteristics of effective and ineffective appraisal:

Ineffective appraisal	Effective appraisal
No clear statement or explanation of purpose of scheme	Purpose clearly defined and explained to managers and staff
A narrow focus, primarily on the assessment of past performance	A wide focus – past performance, future objectives, work-based aims, personal development
Perceived as imposed by top management and additional to 'normal' work	A process discussed with appraisers and appraisees and perceived by them as an integral part of normal management
Administratively complex, with completion of forms and reports becoming an end in itself	Administration and paperwork kept to basic minimum, and seen simply as a helpful aid
Appraisees' perception is of an inquisitorial or fault-finding process	Appraisees see the process as helpful to them in developing their skills and careers
Inadequate preparation by appraisers and appraisees, leading to desultory appraisal discussion	Both parties prepare for appraisal to ensure good use of the opportunity to discuss issues of immediate and long term importance
A one-way process, dominated by appraiser	A two-way process, with appraisee encouraged to self-assess and to comment on appraiser's management style
Discussion limited to performance against a limited number of specific targets	Discussion covers all aspects of the job – targets plus standing elements ('the whole person in the whole job')
Discussion limited to work-based factors	Discussion covers work-based factors (the job), plus the appraisee's personal training and development needs
Discussion dominated by its possible pay outcome	Pay considerations excluded from discussion

Targets set without adequate discussion of action needed to secure achievement	Targets always linked to action plans – i.e. 'what are we aiming for' (target) 'how we are going to achieve it' (action plan)
All or some records kept confidential to management	All records seen by appraisee with opportunity for comment
No vetting by senior management of fairness or consistency of assessments	Managers' assessments of their staff monitored by managers' seniors

Consideration needs also to be given to team performance and appraisal, for work in which the contribution of each individual is heavily dependent on collaboration within a group. It is unsatisfactory to ignore the interdependence of team members when appraising individuals, though attention does need to be given to the possibly varying quality of each member's contribution to team results.

Little mention has been made in this section of performance-related pay (PRP) and there is research evidence that the effective operation of a performance management system – including performance appraisal – is not necessarily dependent on the inclusion of performance pay. Differences of view on this issue are dealt with in Section 6. Here, it should be noted that there is general agreement that the appraisal process can be damaged if it is seen by appraisees as being concerned mainly with the determination of performance pay. Some separation in time periods between the appraisal discussion and any announcement about performance pay is recommended by many practitioners.

Quality management

In the pursuit of quality, two main approaches can be

identified which are sometimes seen as alternatives but are better recognised as complementary:

- quality assurance (QA), including BS 5750 certification
- total quality management

QA and BS 5750
The emphasis in the quality assurance approach is on the design, documentation and operation of procedures to ensure all activities are undertaken in ways which will secure the required quality standards. This implies that the organisation has first decided what its quality standards should be – and this should be related to decisions about the performance indicators described earlier in this section.

Independent assessment of an organisation's quality procedures is not essential to effective quality management, but acquiring certification to the British Standard 5750 (or its international equivalent ISO 9000) is increasingly being demanded of external contractors. In-house contractor units (including some personnel or training functions) are also obtaining 5750 certification, partly to match their external competitors, partly to improve their standing within their organisations.

BS 5750 does not of itself guarantee a high standard of quality – it certifies only that the organisation operates procedures which secure *consistency* of quality, and that these procedures include records of quality performance and are subject to periodic review. It is likely, however, that most organisations with BS certification have set high standards and see their quality procedures as the means of ensuring these standards are maintained. Obtaining certification can be a lengthy and expensive process, as it requires a fundamental review and documentation of every procedure, the probable addition of new procedures to record faults and complaints (and the action taken to rectify these flaws), the production of a quality manual, and assessment by a BS awarding organisation – followed by further periodic assessments to retain the certificate.

Personnel and training departments which have obtained BS 5750 have pointed to two factors which need to be kept in mind:

- Procedures on their own do not always guarantee high quality standards: for example, systematic selection is not necessarily good selection.
- There are situations in which rigid adherence to procedures is detrimental. In one organisation, the personnel unit has included in its set of BS procedures, a process for departing from normal procedure when it is evident this will achieve better results.

Total quality management (TQM)
The TQM approach can be characterised by the priority it gives to attitudes or organisational culture. In essence, the aim of a TQM organisation is to generate enthusiasm and commitment throughout the entire workforce, not just to maintaining high quality, but also to a continuous search for improvement. Quality is secured not by inspection after the event, but by every employee taking full personal responsibility for doing everything well, all the time.

In practical terms, a TQM programme needs to include:

- commitment from top management
- the widespread and continuous promotion of quality as an all-pervading value
- a recognition that this requires a cultural change
- a framework of quality systems which put the emphasis on doing things the right way, first time (i.e. not on error correction but on error prevention)

- The genuine involvement of the whole workforce, perhaps through the operation of quality circles.

Some organisations have attempted but failed to establish a TQM environment. Three reasons for this are:

- cynicism among the workforce about the sincerity of the programme, if quality slogans are not backed by managerial support or adequate resources
- resistance by lower levels of management, if the programme is perceived as being top-driven with a view to empowering employees at large to take more control and so require less supervision
- a failure to amend conventional working procedures, or to introduce the necessary framework of systems to match the new TQM approach.

This last point shows that, to be effective, the TQM approach needs to include at least some elements of QA and should not be seen as a wholly different approach. Quality will not be secured by procedures alone if there is not a culture of commitment: equally, enthusiasm for quality will not secure consistency of achievement without the support of appropriate procedures.

The personnel function has an important role to play in the creation of a quality culture, as the generation of commitment is heavily dependent on effective employee communication, while high standards also require high levels of competence. Particular questions for the personnel manager to address are:

- Is the quality message being adequately communicated and explained throughout the workforce?
- Has everyone had adequate training in the operation of the relevant procedures, and in the skills necessary within their jobs?

- Are quality objectives incorporated in the performance management system?
- Are there any barriers (organisational, attitudinal, procedural) to the achievement of a quality culture?

Finally, does the personnel function itself provide a quality model in its own activities and in the quality of the services it provides to its internal customers?

Section 6
Reward management

Historically, public sector organisations have paid relatively little attention to reward management, as pay and benefits have been determined by national agreements. These agreements have left some scope for local interpretation, but few managers have had to handle the design and negotiation of complete systems of pay and conditions.

Over the past few years, this position has changed significantly towards local pay determination. Reasons include:

- Skills shortages in the latter half of the 1980s, which led to local pressures for more attractive pay and conditions than many national agreements provided.
- A recognition that standardised national pay systems are not compatible with widely varying organisation structures, operational priorities and productivity levels.
- Strong Government pressure to abandon national pay as a matter of political and economic principle.

- Market testing and CCT, which have led to a view that in some functions (e.g. cleaning and catering) nationally negotiated conditions will price the in-house contractor out of the market.

Four aspects of reward management are of particular relevance:

- the pros and cons of national v. local pay determination – and how to implement a change from a national to a local system
- the design of a local pay system
- the pros and cons of performance-related pay, and variants of PRP
- the concept of the employment package, and of flexibility in the provision of benefits.

National v. local pay determination

The case for local pay determination is based on two main arguments:

- That the management of rewards is a positive element of total human resource management, and not just an administrative payroll process. The emphasis is on *local* pay, because local institutions (e.g. individual health trusts, grant maintained schools, local authorities or civil service agencies) each have their own unique local characteristics which need to be reflected in their pay systems.
- That employment costs represent the largest single cost factor, and that local managements cannot exercise effective cost control when this major element of expenditure is determined by the outcome of national negotiations. The devolution of accountability to local unit

managers cannot be fully achieved without including devolution of authority to determine local pay.

These arguments may appear to be overwhelmingly supportive of local pay – yet fully local pay systems are still in the minority. Several reasons (apart from inertia) can be suggested:

- 'Going local' involves a major cultural change both for managers and the workforce, and this needs lengthy and careful planning and preparation.
- Experience and skills in the design, negotiation and management of reward systems are in short supply.
- There are potential legal and industrial relations problems to be resolved in effecting a change from national to local pay.
- Going local does not necessarily achieve cost savings – at least in the first instance. There may be a price to pay (in terms of more attractive terms) in order to secure trade union and/or employee acceptance.
- There is a potential problem in introducing local pay while a national pay system (or a national pay review body) continues to exist. While a national system still exists, organisations going local will be expected by staff and unions to better it – why else should they accept the change?

There is also a question as to whether employees in some occupations are ever likely to accept the differences in pay which will occur between similar institutions if each pursues its own pay policy. These are jobs with the following characteristics:

- The employees have a very strong sense of national occupational identity.

- This identity is institutionalised through high levels of membership of trade unions specific to the occupations concerned.
- The nature of the work and the way it is organised does not vary greatly between different local units.

The fire service provides an example. Firefighters have a strong sense of occupational identity cutting across the geographical boundaries of the various fire authorities. Their trade union (the FBU) is specific to the service and has very high membership levels. The work is very similar in every location. These inhibiting factors do not apply to organisations (such as some Civil Service executive agencies) in which the work and the occupations involved are unique to a single institution.

There is no right answer to the question about local pay. Each organisation needs to analyse its own characteristics and those of its workforce, and to take account of the relevant national situation, before a sound decision can be made. That said, none of the potential difficulties of adopting a local solution wholly offset the disadvantages of not being able either to design a rewards strategy to support local needs, or to exercise some control over a very large cost element.

Some managements are keen to abandon adherence to national pay systems, but are unsure how to effect the change. It is certainly not a simple matter of imposing new terms unilaterally. If employees objected to such action, they could probably sue for breach of contract, or leave and claim constructive dismissal. There are four legally acceptable methods:

- To negotiate an agreement for a new local pay system with the relevant trade unions and for the terms to be incorporated into individual contracts – provided existing contracts make provision for such incorporation.

- If this is not possible, to offer the terms of the new local system to employees individually and hope for a high acceptance rate.
- Within certain conditions (explained below), to terminate all existing contracts with due notice and offer re-engagement on the new terms.
- To apply the new local terms only to newly recruited staff.

The first approach is dependent on the terms of employees' existing contracts including a clause to the effect that:

> Your terms and conditions of employment may be altered from time to time to include the terms of locally negotiated agreements with . . . *the relevant trade union(s)* . . .

The problem for many organisations is that clauses of this kind refer only to *national* collective agreements. In these cases, one of the other methods has to be used.

Offering new, local terms individually to a large workforce may seem a very unsatisfactory way of implementing a new pay system. It involves considerable administrative effort and cannot be guaranteed to result in 100 per cent acceptance. However, it is a method which a number of organisations have used successfully. Factors to consider include:

- the need for an extensive campaign to ensure all staff are fully informed about the new terms
- the extent to which the new terms can be promoted as an improvement on existing national conditions – or

whether a one-off inducement to accept the terms is justified

- whether the trade union(s) can be persuaded, if not to abandon their opposition in principle, at least to avoid any action which might prejudice employees' free choices
- the policy to adopt towards any staff who fail to accept the new terms. (Contractually, it may be necessary to continue to apply in full all the terms of the national agreements to these staff, including future pay awards.)
- whether it would be acceptable, even if not desirable, to have staff employed on two sets of conditions (i.e. local terms for those who accept, national terms for others). Several local authorities have found no real difficulty in operating this way with a 90–95 per cent acceptance rate, particularly as non-acceptances tend to be in the age group nearing retirement. Acceptance rates of only, say, 50 per cent would cause far more difficulty.

The *termination of all current contracts* (with due notice) and the offer of re-engagement on new terms is not a course of action to be embarked on lightly, and is difficult to recommend as a matter of good employment practice. It carries the risks of strong trade union and employee reaction, and could lead to claims for unfair dismissal. It is, however, legally acceptable provided the organisation is able potentially to convince an Industrial Tribunal that there were reasonable grounds for taking such action.

Placing only new employees on the new local terms, while continuing to apply national conditions to existing employees, has major disadvantages, even though it carries less risks than some of the other methods. It could be decades before all current staff have left or retired, and a lengthy period during which employees doing the same work are paid on two different bases is not a recipe for good employee relations.

A halfway position between fully local and fully national conditions is strongly supported by some employers. This is for a national system to continue but for it to provide flexibility in its local application. This can be provided in three ways:

- The system may provide little more than a ladder or 'spinal column' of pay values, from which local managements can construct their own local grades.
- The allocation of jobs to salary grades may be left entirely for local decision, so similar jobs in different organisations may be graded differently. (Problems may arise relating to equal pay legislation if such variances occur in the establishments of a single employer.)
- For non-pay benefits (e.g. holidays, sick pay), the national conditions prescribe only minimum entitlements, which employers are free to better locally.

In such systems, there is still one important national element – the size of the annual pay award. This is a major disadvantage for those local employers who wish to link such awards to local productivity measures, or who wish to set changes in pay in the context of local changes to the whole benefits package.

Factors in the design of a local pay system

Should a local pay system apply to all employees, or only to certain groups? There are many examples of local pay being used only for managerial staff or only for job categories which are not catered for in existing national agreements (e.g. NHS health care assistants). A staged approach may allow time for managements to acquire the new skills involved in operating local pay, but to continue for a lengthy period to pay different groups of employees on different bases does not encourage a unified working culture.

What type of pay structure is needed? Should it consist of a ladder of pay scales, or should jobs be evaluated and paid fixed or spot rates? This may well be influenced by whether (and if so, how) performance-related pay is used.

If scales are to be used – how many are needed to span the whole range of jobs? There is a link here with the organisation structure. A simple, flat organisation structure should be matched by a similarly simple structure of pay scales.

If scales are used, how wide a salary span should each cover, and should the scales overlap? Public sector practice has generally been for short butt-ended scales. Private sector practice is for wider scales, often with the top third of each scale overlapping the bottom third of the next higher scale.

If scales are used, how are employees to progress through each scale? The public sector has conventionally used incremental progression – automatic annual increases based solely on service. This approach has come under increasing criticism and is being replaced (in part or in whole) by pay progression based on performance.

How are the values of the pay points or scales to be determined? In other words, how is the pay structure to be priced? A common solution is to use market surveys, so that a decision can be made as to where to pitch the general levels of pay against those for similar occupations in the economy at large. Alternatively, a policy decision may be needed as to where to pitch local salaries against previous national pay levels.

How are individual jobs to be valued and allocated to scales or pay points? Standard national job descriptions are becoming increasingly outdated as organisations restructure conventional working methods and jobs. Some form of job evaluation is consequently needed to provide an equitable way of job grading. It is essential, that this is free of gender or racial bias. Only a job evaluation system which involves the objective assessment and rating of relevant factors (such as competences and responsibility for resources) would be accepted by the courts as non-discriminatory.

How is the whole system to be periodically repriced? The results of inflation and other changes in the job market necessitate adjustments to keep the structure up-to-date. Is there to be an annual pay review which uprates all the pay values in the structure? On what basis is this, or other forms of review, to be conducted? Factors include:

- The frequency of reviews. There is nothing inevitable about doing so annually: indeed, there is a strong case for breaking the conventional annual cycle and conducting reviews only when evidence exists that changes are necessary to maintain a competitive recruitment and retention position.
- A periodic market pay survey to decide how the structure should be repriced.
- A periodic survey of other organisations' pay settlements, with a view to keeping broadly in step – though there is a trend away from an over-reliance on this concept of 'the going rate' as this fails to take account of local factors and is inherently inflationary.
- Shadowing movements in the retail price index and/or in the national average earnings index. Similar comments apply here as to the going rate – though some regard clearly needs to be given to broad economic and pay trends.

Pay negotiations in a highly unionised environment have a significant influence on pay levels. But even if a system of annual pay negotiations is maintained, it is still essential for managements to have a clear view of their pay objectives, and for these objectives to be based on a thorough assessment of the internal and external factors influencing pay levels.

Performance-related pay (PRP)

There have been two major influences leading to the introduction of various forms of PRP in recent years:

- PRP has been strongly promoted by central government, partly as a matter of political principle, partly as an element in the Citizens Charter. Some government grants (e.g. to higher education institutions) have been dependent on PRP being introduced.
- Independently, many managements have concluded that PRP contributes to improved individual and organisational performance.

That said, many managers still have doubts about the practicability and efficacy of PRP. Some of the main arguments for and against PRP are:

For	Against
PRP engenders a greater awareness among employees of the importance of achieving high standards of performance, and encourages performance improvement	Money is not an effective motivator, particularly in jobs in which employees are motivated by a sense of vocation

A PRP scheme encourages managers to set and monitor high performance and quality standards	It is difficult to set and measure objective performance targets for those involving largely qualitative characteristics
PRP provides more attractive salary opportunities for high performers, and so contributes to recruitment and retention	PRP is divisive, and inhibits the development of a team spirit and collaborative working
It is unfair in a non-PRP environment for employees doing the same work to be paid the same, when some are outstanding performers and others barely adequate	There is little or no research evidence to show that PRP improves performance
The award of a performance payment is an act of recognition, and it is this recognition which is the motivator, not the amount of the payment	Performance payments will motivate only if they are very large, relative to basic pay. The public sector cannot afford large payments

Organisations must decide for themselves the extent to which they agree or disagree with these various views. They should be influenced, however, by the experience (good and bad) of organisations which already operate PRP, not least because some failings of PRP can be attributed to poor systems, rather than to the basic principles.

Features of successful and unsuccessful schemes are summarised in the following schedule:

Successful schemes	**Unsuccessful schemes**
PRP is part of, or supplementary to, a well-designed pay structure	PRP is used to boost earnings to a reasonable level in an inadequate pay structure
Performance criteria for PRP are clearly defined and understood by all staff	Payment criteria are not well-defined, or are not understood by staff

Assessments of performance for PRP are objective and not influenced by irrelevant personality factors	PRP assessments are biased by personal and subjective views (i.e. likes and dislikes) of individual managers
PRP criteria reinforce organisational values and goals	PRP criteria conflict with other of the organisation's values or goals
Staff understand how performance payments are calculated	Staff are uncertain as to how payments are calculated
Payments are made on the basis of assessments of total performance (the whole job)	Payments are made only for achievement of certain targets, thus favouring staff working on projects as opposed to those doing on-going work
Assessments and the distribution of payments is consistent across the whole organisation	The standard of assessments and the distribution of payments is inconsistent across the organisation
No alterations are made to performance assessments simply to produce a set financial outcome	Assessments are changed to produce pre-determined financial outcomes
PRP is applied to whole staff groups	PRP is limited to certain jobs, so the scheme is seen as favouring some staff more than others

Once it has been decided to introduce PRP, the following issues need to be considered:

- How performance assessments are to be made. Normally, these are based on the views managers reach after conducting performance appraisals, although it is best not to discuss payments in the course of the appraisal discussions.
- How performance is to be categorised. The appraisal

70

will probably produce different ratings for different aspects of the job. For PRP, these must be incorporated into one overall rating, using a scale such as:

- outstanding: all targets met and many exceeded, plus all-round excellence in every aspect of the job
- very good: all targets met, and good overall job performance
- satisfactory: key targets and most others met; fully acceptable overall job performance
- not fully satisfactory: some key targets missed, and some improvement needed in other aspects of general job performance
- not satisfactory: many targets missed and need for significant improvement in other aspects of job performance
- not yet assessable (e.g. recent recruits or transferees)

There is an argument for four or six category rating scales to avoid the tendency for ratings to cluster at the mid-point.

- What form the payments should take (see below).
- Whether there should be an appeal process for employees with grievances about their assessments. There is a case for considering grievances about the way assessments have been carried out, but not for appeals against the outcome when it is evident that the assessment has been undertaken properly.
- How to 'sell' the PRP scheme to managers, employees and trade unions. An extensive information and consultation exercise has preceded the introduction of successful schemes. PRP will not be effective if the managers who have to operate it doubt its validity, or if staff are suspicious or antagonistic.

The main variants in the types of performance payments are:

- Salary progression within defined pay scales. Employees progress through their pay scales on the basis of performance assessments, not by automatic incremental progression. High performers progress more rapidly than others. Poor performers may stay on the scale minima. Pay scales need to be wide enough to allow for significant progression by high performers before they reach the scale maxima, so maxima may need to be 30 per cent or more above minima.
- Salary progression above normal scale maxima for high performers. This approach is usually based on somewhat basic salary scales, but will provide for an additional performance range above normal maxima. Progression within the short basic scales may continue to be by conventional service increments.
- Lump sums, paid separately from salary. The basic pay structure may be either fixed point salaries (i.e. no scales), or short incremental scales. The size of lump sum performance payments may be expressed either as percentages of salary, defined sums, or the equivalent of one or more increments.
- A combination of salaried performance progression and lump sums. A disadvantage of salary progression, whether within or above basic scales, is that consistent high performers eventually reach a salary maximum, so that further high performance cannot be rewarded. For this reason, some schemes operate salary progression on a performance basis within the salary scales, but pay lump sums to high performers who have reached their salary maxima.

A more fundamental approach combines performance

payments with the general annual pay award. The organisation determines the overall increase it considers justifiable for normally satisfactory employees and as a general adjustment to pay values, say, 5 per cent. Individual increases are then built around this figure, dependent on performance assessments, e.g.:

- outstanding: 10 per cent
- very good: 7 per cent
- satisfactory: 5 per cent
- not fully satisfactory: 2 per cent
- unsatisfactory: Nil

This method is best suited to structures using fixed point salaries rather than scales.

One issue which often causes difficulty is that of budgeting for PRP. To keep the costs within budgeted limits some organisations imposed forced distributions of performance ratings. Managers will be told that they cannot assess more than, say, 5 per cent of employees as outstanding performers or 20 per cent as very good performers. While these proportionate distributions may be reasonably accurate across the whole range of a large workforce, they can produce very unsatisfactory effects if imposed on small sections. The credibility of the whole scheme will be destroyed if employees discover that the number of high performance ratings is influenced by an arbitrary 'ration'.

There are more acceptable ways of keeping costs under control:

- Effective training and monitoring of managers' assessments can go a long way towards ensuring consistency and preventing unwarranted skewing of assessments.
- For schemes using either the lump sum approach, or salary additions which are not tied to predetermined

incremental steps, a budgeted sum can be allocated for performance payments. An unexpectedly large proportion of high performance assessments will then mean that the individual sums paid are less than would otherwise occur – but the assessments themselves do not have to be altered.

The employment package

From a cost and motivational viewpoint, salaries need to be treated as only one element in a whole package of conditions and benefits. In a local system, there may be trade-offs between salaries and some other benefits. On a cost benefit basis, too, it is the total cost and impact of the whole employment package which needs to be considered – not just salaries. Additionally, there is scope for:

- benefits which have not previously been provided within national conditions
- flexibility in individual employees' choice of benefits.

Staff shortages at one time led to the extensive introduction of benefits previously particular to the private sector – e.g. private medical insurance, cars and mortgage subsidies. Recent experience indicates that there are dangers in the ad hoc introduction of such benefits simply to ease short-term recruitment and retention problems. Once these problems diminish, the considerable costs of such benefits come under scrutiny, yet to withdraw them causes adverse staff reaction. A more considered approach should take account of trends in taxation, total employment costs, and the overall features of the whole package relative to longer-term employment objectives.

This long-term view pays attention to the effect of various

benefits on the organisation's resourcing and equal opportunity policies, and may show that the introduction of benefits such as:

- childcare assistance (allowances, vouchers, creches)
- career break schemes
- welfare and stress counselling services
- health promotion facilities
- grants to assist employees with personal studies

would be far more beneficial than status-linked benefits such as free medical insurance or prestige cars for senior managers.

One important benefit which has received very little local attention in the past is pensions. With pension scheme membership no longer compulsory, some organisations may find it of benefit to offer alternatives to the national schemes – particularly for recruits who may have their own personal pensions. Legislation may be necessary before many public sector organisations could operate their own schemes, but there may not be any statutory bar on contributing the equivalent of the employer's contributions to an employee's own money-purchase personal pension plan. Expert pensions and tax advice is essential, however, before any new pension arrangements are introduced.

The provision of 'cafeteria benefits' (i.e. some freedom of individual choice of benefits) is worth serious attention. The real value of the same benefit to different employees varies considerably depending on individual circumstances. For example, it is a waste of money to provide family medical cover for employees whose spouses work for other employers who also provide this benefit.

There are two broad approaches to flexible benefits:

- flexibility within individual benefits
- flexibility of choice between at least some benefits.

The three main benefits within which flexibility is most common are attendance times, cars and pensions:

- Flexible working hours have been discussed in Section 4.
- When leased cars are provided, the employee can be given three choices:
  - to choose any available vehicle for a set annual leasing cost
  - to choose a more expensive vehicle and pay the extra leasing cost
  - to choose a less expensive vehicle and take the unspent proportion of the leasing allowance in cash.

- The basic choice in pensions is whether or not to join. Some schemes, however, also provide a choice of contribution level (say, between 3 per cent and 6 per cent of salary) to give different levels of benefit. All schemes must offer the choice of additional pension benefits paid for by AVCs (additional voluntary contributions). Not all schemes publicise this option sufficiently, bearing in mind that it is the most tax-effective way for employees to boost their pension entitlements.

Flexibility of choice *between* certain benefits is more fundamental. Examples are:

- Offering extra salary instead of a car – this cash for car option is becoming increasingly popular as tax changes erode the tax advantages of the 'company car'.
- Providing a variety of permutations of life insurance, private medical insurance, permanent health insurance, pension benefits and the like. The principle is that an

employee opting out of, say, medical insurance, may choose to have the equivalent cost allocated to the employer's contribution to his or her pension provision.

- A few organisations are additionally allowing some trade-offs between salary, sick pay or annual leave. Up to, say, five days extra annual leave can be 'bought' from salary; or five fewer days than standard offset by additional salary.

A flexible benefit scheme involving a wide range of benefits requires careful costing and close attention to the tax implications. While the principle is simple (i.e. any benefits from those on offer can be chosen which together cost the employer a defined total sum), the factors to consider are:

- What degree of flexibility might be provided? (For example, it would be wholly unsatisfactory to permit a trading-in of all annual leave, or the 'purchase' of too large an addition.)
- Might a major trend in employee choices change the unit costs of the benefit concerned? (For example, per capita medical insurance premiums will rise if only the older age groups opt to stay in the scheme.)
- What arrangements will exist for employees to change their choice of benefits as time passes? Some organisations limit this to a once-a-year option.

Finally, an organisation which is taking full control of its own rewards system should consider the possibility of harmonising its pay and benefits across all employee groups. The major differences in benefits between blue-collar and white-collar employees (usually to the detriment of the former) militates against the creation of a unified organisational culture and collaborative working attitudes. There is no justification in logic or equity for an experienced and long-service mechanic, driver or cook to have to work longer hours and have less holiday and poorer sick pay than a newly recruited and inexperienced filing clerk – yet such imbalances are common in many parts of the public sector.

There are two factors which inhibit moves towards harmonisation (or single status).

- *Cost.* Uprating manual employee's benefits can be expensive. So a harmonisation programme will probably need to be phased in over a period of years, and linked to measures to improve productivity.
- *Attitudes.* Some managers and staff (and their trade unions) are defensive of the apparently higher status of the white-collar worker, and will use the cost argument to delay any move towards harmonisation. Only a programme of explanation and discussion is likely to change these views, and in some cases a bold decision by top management will be needed to take the first step on the road to single status, regardless of latent resistance.

There are fewer attitudinal difficulties in harmonising terms between various professional groups, and this may be a sensible way of starting the harmonisation process.

Section 7
Training and development

The public sector has a comparatively good training record when set against the generality of UK industry – though the UK as a whole falls behind the levels of training achieved by many of our EC partners. However, public sector training has had several characteristics which do not fully meet current needs:

- The emphasis has been on formal training to acquire professional qualifications rather than job-related skills, or on administrative (rather than managerial) skills.
- Most training has been by attendance at off-the-job courses – generally the most expensive training method.
- Training activities have not always been co-ordinated, set within the strategic framework of the organisation's 'business plan', or related to national initiatives such as the National Vocational Qualifications (NVQ) or Management Charter Initiative (MCI).

There are consequently three aspects of training which have a particular relevance to most public sector organisations:

- training to develop the new job-related skills and competences required to cope effectively with all the trends outlined in Section 1
- the use of other and possibly more cost-effective forms of training than off-the-job courses – and the concept of the learning organisation
- the local and national strategic context in which training should be set.

Training for new skills

Each organisation will have its own specific training needs, related to its particular function. Most of these needs will be among 'front-line' staff – those directly concerned with service delivery. There are, however, two aspects which are relevant to all organisations:

- training in new management skills
- developing a multi-skilled workforce.

In almost every part of the public sector, managers need to develop their knowledge and expertise in handling the new responsibilities and functions which result from devolution. There are also the new quasi-commercial skills involved in operating. The subjects in which managers are likely to need training can be grouped under four main headings:

Managing people	Managing finance
Recruitment and selection	Costing functions and services
Handling discipline and grievances	Operating trading accounts
Staff leadership and motivation	Budgetary control
Staff appraisal	Managing a cost centre
Managing reward systems	Managing cash flow
Trade union relations	Controlling overheads

80

Equal opportunities and negotiation	**Managing a 'business'**
Employment legislation	
Health and safety	Business planning
	Customer orientation
	Performance management
Managing information	Quality management
	Producing specifications
Management information systems	Service level agreements
Principles of IT	Letting and vetting tenders
IT strategies	Managing contractors
	Commercial negotiation
	Marketing

The emphasis is on the skills involved in managing people and business units (or cost centres). Underpinning these aspects is the effective use of information and skilful financial management.

For employees below management level, the main general training need is the broadening of expertise beyond the traditionally narrow boundaries of closely defined professional or technical occupations. Flexibility in the workforce is aided by staff having a wide range of ability to take on different tasks. The extent to which it is possible to achieve multi-skilling is dependent on the particular characteristics and technology of each organisation, but the principle can be adopted as a training objective by almost all organisations. A few very simple examples might be:

- training delivery drivers in stores procedures and stores employees in driving, in order to obtain an interchangeable depot workforce.
- developing a general purpose team trained to cover office security, cleaning, portering and driving
- training secretaries in accounting procedures, research techniques and other skills to enable them to provide wide-ranging support well beyond conventional office duties.

More imaginative possibilities exist in many professional fields, but these are matters for each organisation to identify in the light of their own particular functions.

Cost-effective training methods

Off-the-job training courses, though forming the backbone of most training programmes, have three potential disadvantages:

- Externally run courses are often very expensive, and a minority of employees sent on such courses can soon use up the whole of an organisation's training budget.
- With staffing levels reduced to the minimum for cost reasons, it has become increasingly difficult for organisations to release staff for course attendances.
- People differ in their learning styles, and not all staff learn best in the formal course setting.

In considering what other forms of training might be used, it is helpful to think of training as learning – that is, as an activity which is dependent on the active involvement of the person being trained. This view corrects a tendency to consider the trainer as the active partner in a relationship in which the trainee is a passive recipient of knowledge. In reality, people learn from a whole range of experiences, whether or not such learning is conscious or intended, and there is research evidence that the most powerful form of learning is actual work experience.

Before examining how work-based learning (and other non-course activities) can form a significant part of a training strategy, one reservation must be registered. This is that these methods apply mainly to employees as individuals. Conventional training courses may be unavoidable if it is necessary for staff to learn in groups. Course costs can then be contained either by running courses in-house with the organisation's own staff as tutors, or by bringing external tutors into the organisation rather than sending employees to external training centres.

Work-based learning can make use of a variety of activities as listed below. The aim should be for managers to identify or create these learning opportunities and so use them positively, instead of such learning being largely accidental:

- *Work allocation.* Much can often be done within the normal allocation of work tasks to broaden employees' knowledge and experience. Managers sometimes develop a habit of always giving certain tasks to the same person. If instead, tasks are shared, more employees will be helped to widen their expertise.
- *Being a member of a working party or project team.* Employees can be allocated to such teams not just for the contribution they can make to the teams' objectives, but also as a planned learning experience.
- *Chairing or leading a working party or project team.* This can be a useful learning experience for an employee who has not yet had a leadership or co-ordinating opportunity.
- *Job swaps or job rotation.* Two employees can be invited to exchange jobs for a set period (say, six months) so that each broadens their knowledge and experience. More generally, employees in a multi-task team can be rotated through all the jobs involved, so that, in time, everyone in the team is capable of doing every job.
- *Secondments.* Temporary postings can be made within the organisation with the specific purpose of improving an employee's knowledge and skills; secondments to other organisations may be an even more powerful way

of widening an employee's professional or managerial horizons.

- *Mentoring.* An experienced and competent employee may be asked to act as a mentor for a less experienced colleague, and generally provide guidance and help with development during a learning period.
- *Coaching.* All managers can help to develop their staff by using every possible opportunity within normal work routines to explain, instruct and encourage. Managers sometimes overlook the extent to which even the most informal short discussion (perhaps in which the reason for a new task is explained, or a question is asked about 'any problems?') can contribute to an employee's learning.
- *Networking.* Staff can be encouraged to establish a network of contacts with colleagues in other departments, or with fellow professionals with other local employers. They can share common problems, learn from each other, and be a source of informal, individual assistance and mentoring. They may also arrange lunch-time discussion groups or other out-of-hours learning activities.

To gain maximum benefit from work-based learning, it is important that the learning opportunities and objectives in each event are identified in advance and discussed between the manager and employee concerned – before, during and on conclusion of each experience.

Two other forms of individual training which do not involve attendance at training courses, and which are forming an increasingly large component of some organisations' training strategies, are:

- *Distance learning.* It is now possible to study almost any topic by some form of self-learning package, usually involving workbooks, guided reading, videos and cassettes, plus in some cases telephone tutoring and weekend or summer schools. Packages range from short, single-subject material, equivalent to the content of conventional two or three week training courses, to Masters degrees involving several years study.

- *Computer based training programmes.* The employee learns by following a course of study on a PC, keying in answers to questions which test the extent to which learning has occurred.

Some organisations make material of these kinds available on loan to any employee who wishes to study. PC-based training packages can also be set up in an office location where employees can drop in during lunch breaks or after work for short periods of study.

These last two forms of training are more effective in developing knowledge than skills; and the individuals concerned need to be strongly self-motivated. This motivation can be aided, however, by providing support and encouragement, including providing work experience to give practical insight into the subjects under study.

The whole training/learning process can also be aided by developing the concept that employees should take ownership of their own development – a particularly important factor for those who are members of professional institutes, such as the IPM, which are requiring evidence of continuous professional development (CPD) as a criterion for continued membership. Employees can be encouraged to keep individual training logs in which they record their personal development objectives and learning experiences. Additionally, some organisations are introducing 'development contracts' in which the employee and the organisation commit themselves to joint action to achieve improvements in knowledge and competence.

There is also a broader aspect than the development of individuals – the concept of the learning organisation. This implies an awareness among all managers that the organisation as a whole needs to learn from its experience and adapt its approach accordingly. In the private sector, business failures have often resulted from failure to learn and adapt sufficiently quickly to changes in customer preferences or among the competition. Public sector bodies may experience the same type of difficulty, particularly when they are exposed to market testing. Reviewing the organisation's progress, problems, failures and successes, in order to identify strengths, weaknesses, opportunities and threats (the well-known SWOT analysis), should be a standing item on management team agendas.

Training in context

To be most effective, training activities need to be placed in the context of an organisation-wide training strategy. This should take account of:

- the individual training needs identified through the appraisal process
- the collective training needs indicated by the objectives in the organisation's operational or business plan
- the most cost-effective training methods to meet the needs which have been identified
- national training trends and initiatives which would help to meet the organisation's training and resourcing objectives.

Part of the appraisal process should be the consideration of each employee's training and development needs. These can be categorised as:

- the immediate training required to help the employee perform more effectively in the current job
- training to develop the employee's potential to undertake other, and possibly more advanced, work or to prepare for promotion.

One task for the personnel function is periodically to collate all the individual training needs identified in the appraisal process to see if there are gaps in the collective training programmes, or if trends exist which point to the need for new training initiatives.

Unless an organisation undertakes some form of forward planning (commonly in the form of a business plan), it is almost impossible for it to identify its overall training needs. Business plans, regularly up-dated, should address the questions:

- Will the achievement of the organisation's aims require changes in the range or type of skills among our employees?
- If so, what are these changes and what training will be needed to ensure the necessary skills are developed?

Training plans should be an integral element of the business plan – not something thought about at a later date after skills shortages have emerged.

The relationship between the organisation's training activities and national trends and initiatives is also important. Employees will benefit from local training which leads to recognised national qualifications: the organisation will benefit by drawing on concepts, material and resources which have been designed to meet the needs of employers generally.

In particular, organisations need to be fully aware of relevant developments in NVQs, and to know about the availability of NVQ training material and courses. Sources of information are the local Training and Enterprise Council (TEC) and the various national employers organisations. In the management field, organisations may also find the work of the Management Charter Initiative of considerable value. The NVQ and MCI movements share the same emphasis on job-related competencies and the use of a wide variety of training and learning methods which this section has discussed.

Section 8
Employee relations

Traditionally, in the public sector, nationally negotiated collective agreements have regulated the formal relationships between employers and employees, even for top management positions. There has also been a historically high level of employee membership of the nationally recognised trade unions. Employee relations have consequently had two characteristics which are now being called into question:

- Local industrial relations arrangements have been set by, and mirror, the national systems, rather than local circumstances.
- Employer/employee relations have in the main been seen as involving managers and trade union representatives, as distinct from employees at large.

There are several factors which now indicate a need for most public sector employers to review fundamentally their whole approach to collective and individual relations with trade unions and employees:

- Devolution is weakening, if not disbanding, the role of national negotiations. The move towards local pay bargaining is only one element of this trend.
- Historically similar units are now adopting different structures, styles and strategies, so standardised patterns of employee relations are no longer appropriate.
- In some parts of the country in some public services, trade union membership has fallen to levels well below 50 per cent, so employers can no longer be confident that the unions are reflecting the views of the generality of employees.
- Recent legislation has weakened the trade unions' potential negotiating power and is inhibiting traditional 'spheres of influence' agreements between trade unions which in the past have led to single unions maintaining a dominant position within a particular workplace or service.
- Changes in trade union organisation (such as the creation of UNISON from a merger of NALGO, NUPE and COHSE) require changes to previous industrial relations arrangements.
- There is a growing recognition that *all* employees need to be involved in information and communication processes, and that it is not satisfactory to rely on trade union representatives to relay information from managers to employees.

Before deciding what changes to current arrangements are desirable, it is necessary to note several legal points:

- There is no legal process by which trade union recognition can be enforced.
- Employees must be free to join or not join any trade union they choose, and it is unlawful to put pressure on an employee to influence this choice. It is not unlawful,

however, to offer more attractive benefits to employees who opt out of the terms of collective agreements and accept individual contracts.

- The law distinguishes between recognition for collective bargaining purposes (e.g. to negotiate pay and conditions) and recognition for representational purposes (e.g. to assist individual members in disciplinary and grievance cases).
- If trade unions are recognised for collective bargaining, there is a legal requirement to provide them with such relevant information as they need in order to negotiate effectively. This may include data on such matters as average earnings, grading distributions, and the financial state of the organisation.
- There are also legal requirements to consult recognised trade unions about possible redundancies, and about impending transfers of undertakings (e.g. when functions are taken over by private sector contractors).
- Collective agreements are not legally binding unless they specifically state that they are (and this is almost unheard of in the UK).
- The terms of collective agreements may, however, be contractually binding within employees' individual contract of employment, if these terms are incorporated (see also Section 6).

Trade union relations

Bearing these points in mind, there are a number of issues to consider when reviewing what local policy to adopt towards relations with trade unions:

- levels of union membership
- recognition or derecognition

- extent of recognition (i.e. all or only some emloyees)
- multi- or single-union recognition
- collective bargaining or only representational rights
- single table bargaining in a multi-union situation

It is difficult to make satisfactory decisions about possible changes to the industrial relations arrangements without information about the level of union membership among employees. Payroll deductions of union dues may provide some indication – but this needs to be treated with caution as trade unions are increasingly encouraging members to pay by direct debit through their bank accounts. The trade unions may be willing to provide membership information. Alternatively, it may be possible to issue a questionnaire to staff asking for their membership details, although this might well generate adverse reaction unless the reasons are fully explained and the trade unions are prepared to give the exercise their support. Another alternative is to arrange for an independent body (probably the Electoral Reform Society) to conduct a survey and guarantee confidentiality of the individual responses. This is a more likely course of action when combined (perhaps at a later stage) with a ballot to discover the extent of employee support for a change to single union status. Either way, advice from ACAS (the independent advisory and conciliation service) is advisable before embarking on any such surveys.

Membership levels may be so low that the present pattern of union recognition is not considered to be justified. One option is then derecognition, usually involving giving the union(s) concerned reasonable notice (say, six months). Complete derecognition is a very extreme step for a public sector organisation to take against a tradition of full union involvement in local as well as national bargaining and consultation. It should be noted, too, that an announcement about derecognition may well generate fear and suspicion among employees about the employer's motivation. This may then lead to a large-scale upsurge in union membership – and so negate the reason for derecognition. A less extreme option is to consider derecognition for only some categories of staff – with senior management being the most likely group for this action.

Assuming it is decided to continue with some form of recognition, and that changes in the present pattern of union representation are practicable, consideration may be given to the possibility of single union recognition. Some public sector bodies have inherited a situation in which even a small workforce is represented by several recognised unions who may not always agree to work together. The employer may then have to negotiate separately on the same issue with each union, or be adversely affected by inter-union disagreements. Industrial relations are certainly simplified if only one trade union is involved. Whether this is achievable is dependent partly on the membership criteria of the unions involved, and partly on employee and union wishes. It is on this point which an employee ballot may prove helpful – provided this is fairly conducted and, preferably, has the support of the trade unions involved.

An option applying to the recognition of any trade union is whether this extends to full collective bargaining rights, or is only for consultative and/or representational rights. The distinctions are of crucial importance:

- Collective bargaining rights mean that the employer has accepted that changes to pay and conditions (along with other matters such as the facilities to be granted to the union) will be the subject of negotiation and agreement with the union.
- Consultative rights mean that the employer agrees to keep the trade union informed about matters of employee

and union interest, and to have discussions about these matters. However, the employer does not concede a need for negotiation and agreement before implementing changes – only to listen to what the union has to say.

- Representational rights apply to the union's ability to act on behalf of any of its members in an individual capacity: usually, to represent the employee in disciplinary or grievance procedures.

Situations sometimes arise in which a hitherto unrecognised union recruits some employees and then seeks recognition. The employer, however, may not wish to complicate the collective bargaining situation by increasing the number of unions recognised for this purpose. It may then be acceptable to extend only representational rights to the new union, making it clear in writing that this does not imply any right to participate in negotiations on collective issues.

It may prove necessary to recognise several unions for collective bargaining purposes – for example, where the unions' membership criteria prevent any one union from recruiting among all the occupations involved. In these circumstances, it may be possible to obtain the unions' agreement for them to act as a joint trade union side – known as single-table bargaining. This avoids the need for separate negotiation with different unions on the same issue. There are a number of national precedents for such an arrangement, e.g. the national manual workers agreements in local government in which the GMB, TGWU and NUPE form a single trade union side.

For consultative purposes on matters other than pay and conditions, it may also be possible to bring together trade unions which for policy reasons, or because they represent wholly different categories of employees, would not be able to form a single body for collective bargaining.

Some county councils, for example, meet unions representing manual, white-collar, fire service and teaching unions in a single consultative forum to discuss such matters as the authorities' annual budget, equal opportunities, and occupational health.

Relations with employees

Organisations need to develop policies and processes for their relations with employees at large, as distinct from trade union relations. The main aspects to consider (apart from the day-to-day contact between managers and their staff) are:

- the use of individual contracts of employment
- collective employee representation
- employee communication systems.

The disbanding of collective bargaining by a number of organisations – often coincident with the adoption of local pay systems – implies that collective agreements which are not legally binding are replaced by individual contracts which are enforceable at law. In a very small workforce, or for a small number of senior managerial jobs, it is practicable to consider each individual contract as open to individual negotiation. Where large numbers are concerned, particularly of employees doing the same work, the amount of time involved in individual bargaining and the differences in pay and conditions which could result, make truly individual bargaining wholly unrealistic. In practice, large organisations which have disbanded collective bargaining have substituted this with unilateral decision-making on pay and conditions – perhaps ameliorated by consultation (but not negotiation) – with elected employee representatives.

If this form of collectively imposed individual contracts is used, it is important that the contract documentation issued when an employee is recruited includes a phrase along the following lines:

> These terms and conditions are subject to such future changes as . . . *the organisation* . . . may decide from time to time.

Without such a phrase, it would be open to any employee to challenge any change to which he or she objected, as a breach of the original contract. Even with this phrase, a unilateral change which worsened the terms of employment would potentially be open to legal challenge if it was likely that a court would decide the change was unreasonable. One good reason for collective bargaining to be retained in an organisation of any size is that, by incorporation of the terms of agreements into individual contracts, any such complications are avoided.

With or without trade unions, there are circumstances in which it is helpful for managements to be able to meet with elected employee representatives. Consultative discussions cannot be held effectively within mass meetings of all employees, and managers need a channel of contact through which to obtain collective employee views and concerns. A system of consultative committees to which employees are elected from each of the organisation's sections (or occupational categories), regardless of trade union membership, is consequently well worth consideration – particularly if union membership levels are low.

All employees need to be kept fully informed during periods of change and, as change is endemic, this implies a continuous process of employee communication which goes beyond the operation of consultative committees. The components of a compreshensive communication strategy may include:

- briefing groups, conducted by every manager and supervisor with their own groups of employees. To be effective, managers need to be given briefing notes on organisation-wide issues to ensure a consistency of message, and add their own information about matters specific to their groups.
- occasional mass meetings of all employees, addressed by top management on major issues
- staff newsletters or house journals
- noticeboard announcements
- messages included in payroll envelopes to ensure they go to all staff
- staff circulars, also issued to all employees
- annual reports of the organisation's progress and plans.

There may also be situations in which specially produced videos may be produced – for example, to give employees information about a new location to which staff are being asked to transfer.

An effective communications strategy has the objective of ensuring that the workforce is well informed at all times. It should be:

- *Honest*. It will not give biased information or put a managerial or PR gloss on all the news.
- *Comprehensive*. It will relay and explain bad news as well as good, and will not omit issues simply because of possible managerial sensitivity.
- *Timely*. It will use one or other of the communication media to ensure important news is relayed quickly.

Further reading

People Management: Human Resources in Tomorrow's Public Services. Audit Commission: 1991

Personnel: The Agenda for Change. Local Government Management Board: 1989

Changing Culture. A Williams, P Dobson, M Walters: IPM 1989

Handbook of Performance Management. F Neale: IPM 1991

Management of Performance Manual. B Urwin: Longman 1991

Total Quality: Success through People. R Collard: IPM 1989

Modern Quality Management Manual. C Bone: Longman 1991

Reward Management. M Armstrong and H Murlis: IPM 1992

Performance Related Pay. A Fowler: South East Employers Organisation 1988

Essentials of Employment Law. D Lewis: IPM 1990

Law and Employment series. O Aikin (editor): IPM 1993

Training and Development. R Harrison: IPM 1988

Training Interventions. 3rd ed. M Reid, H Barrington and J Kenny: IPM 1992

Management Development. A Mumford: IPM 1989

'How To' series of articles. A Fowler: *Personnel Management Plus,* monthly from July 1990

ACAS Advisory booklets